Texas Foreclosure

Real Estate Investing for Beginners

How to Find, Finance & Buy Homes In Foreclosure

by

Neilson Roberts

Table of Contents

Chapter 1

State of Texas Overview

State of Texas Overview

Tejas or Texas means "friend" comes from the word Taysha' from the Native American language Caddo.

One of the things that makes Texas a great place to be a real estate investor is that the state has a population of 28,701,845 million residents, which ranks second in the United States!

The Texas median household income is $59,206.

Other interesting facts about Texas:

Spoken languages: English, Spanish

Motto: Friendship

State song: Texas, Our Texas

State Nickname: The Lone Star State

State Capital: Austin

Biggest city: Houston

State of Texas Overview

Points of interest in Texas

Here are a few of some of the great places to enjoy yourself in Texas:

1. San Antonio River Walk – San Antonio

2. Space Center - Houston

3. Big Bend National Park

4. Beach - Port Arthur

5. Six Flags Amusement Park – Fiesta

6. Texas wineries – Austin - Fredericksburg

7. Beach - South Padre Island

Best Food

According the the web site The Daily Meal the best 24 hour dinner is Magnolia Cafe in Austin. The best "all you can eat deal" is Allen's Family Style Meals in Sweetwater. Best Burrito: Campechano, El Burrito Wey Estilo Jalisco, San Antonio. Many consider The Salt Lick BBQ, located at the Dallas/Fort Worth International Airport the best barbecue in the state.

State of Texas Overview

The Texas Economy

Any business person, especially a real estate investor, wants to have a business where the customer base has plenty of money. Another thing that makes Texas a fantastic place to be an investor is it's 1.8 trillion dollar economy, which is the second highest in the United States. Texas has a gross domestic product higher than the Countries of Canada, Spain and Russia just to name a few...

The 2019 unemployment rate in Texas was 3.8 percent, compared to the United States national average of 3.6 percent.

Fortune 500 Companies

A few of the Fortune Five Hundred companies based in Texas are AT&T, J.C. Penney, Whole Foods Market and Tenet Healthcare.

Billionaires in Texas

According to Forbes magazine there are 56 billionaires living in Texas.

So there is plenty of money to be made in Texas and it is your job as an investor, to make sure as much as possible finds it's way to your bank account.

.

Chapter 2

How To Purchase Investment Property

Expert Strategies to Purchase Property

Expert Strategies to Purchase Property

AVOIDING & MANAGING & ELIMINATING RISK

Legendary Real Estate investor Dave Del Dotto once said "stick with the government, they will make you rich.". Real Estate is one of the safest investments in the world, when done properly. There is risk just driving to the grocery store. The only thing separating you from a head on collision is a yellow strip of paint. That being said, there are risks in every financial investment decision you make.

Do your research. Know what you want to do, before you begin. Are you looking to flip properties? Hold on and make money on the interest rates? Are you looking for a property to live in? Are you looking to rent out properties? Each decision requires a different type of research. If you are looking to rent out properties then you need to research what the local apartment complexes and homes are renting for in the area. If you are looking to flip a property then you need to find a real estate agent that can give you comps that have sole in the area within the past year.

Visit any property you are going to purchase. You do not want to get stuck with swampland or a unbuildable lot.

Expert Strategies to Purchase Property

AVOIDING & MANAGING & ELIMINATING RISK

You also don't want to get stuck with a property that has high property taxes. Learn the property tax rates of all the counties in the state that you are going to invest in.

Make sure that the property has not been condemned.

Make sure that the property does not have numerous costly violations of city codes.

Ask multiple real estate agents for information on any area you are interested in investing.

Ask about possible environmental issues.

Research possible liens by builders and contractors.

Beware of a owner who may declare bankruptcy on a property. This is a manageable risk but because laws change constantly, consult a real estate attorney for more information on how to handle this risk.

Avoid scams by dealing with government employees as much as possible.

Expert Strategies to Purchase Property

1. Decide how much you can afford to invest and stick with the numbers you come up with. Avoid something called Auction fever. It can be started by a "fast hammer". A fast hammer is when the auctioneer closes the auction early at a amazing price. It is designed to get your attention and get a fever about being the next one in the room to get a "Great Deal". When you go to a auction you should have a list of properties you have research and what your bid is going to be. This will help you to avoid Auction Fever.

2. Research. Single family homes with at least 3 bedrooms are great investments if purchased at the right price. Your research tells you what the right price is. Remember to use real estate agents and their access to the multiple listing service. Also many big companies like Remax and Century 21 have websites up with tons of information on the real estate area you wish to invest in.

www.trulia.com

 www.zillow.com

www.biggerpockets.com

https://www.census.gov/quickfacts/table/PST045216/00

http://www.realtor.org

Those are just a few of the great sites to get research information on real estate.

Expert Strategies to Purchase Property

3. Get in contact with local counties for a list of delinquent properties for sale. Also ask when the sales will take place. Ask if you can be put on a mailing list. Use the internet to track down as much information as you can. Don't be afraid to use search engines other than Google. Bing and Yahoo are also great search engines to use.

4. Buy from other investors. Some people get in over their head. As long as you know the numbers and have research the property, it does not matter who you purchase it from as long as it is a good deal. One investor in Michigan recently purchased every single property for sale at a tax auction. He has to sell those properties or he is responsible for paying the taxes. As Carelton Sheets once said "you can't rationalize murder" so how can you rationalize why someone might offer you a great deal? Just do your due diligence on the property before making a deal.

5. Establish a relationship with local officials. Learn the names of the people who work in government offices that will be giving you information. Visit in person and say thank you. Call and say thank you. Send them a card that says thank you. How many people do you think do that for them? They will remember you. I worked for the government for over 20 years. I still remember the woman who repeatedly gave me lemon-aid when it was hot outside.

Expert Strategies to Purchase Property

6. Buy early in the Year. When you buy a tax lien certificate, back taxes have to be paid to the treasurer as well as interest and penalties. Redeem the property and you could be earning interest on this larger amount of money. If the property is not redeemed you can turn in the tax lien certificate and be handed a deed for the property, any extra amount you pay for the certificate comes from you because you could have gotten the same property for less.

7. Try smaller counties you may have much less competition.

8. Invest in your comfort zone. Try to find mentors who have already done what it is you want to do. As your knowledge and experience increases then you can take on bigger projects.

9. Write down your goals. Remember to answer the question of why you are doing this in the first place. A powerful why will keep you motivated when it comes time to do the legwork required to be successful.

10. Take Action. There are plenty of smart people who are poor. Proper Knowledge plus action is the key to success.

Expert Strategies to Purchase Property

In microeconomics total cost (TC) describes the total economic cost of production and is made up of variable costs, which vary according to the quantity of a good produced and include inputs such as labor and raw materials, plus fixed costs.

In English... you factor in as many external costs, not just the cost of the investment property.

In order to be successful when buying investment property, you have to be good at determining the Total Cost of a property.

11. Get Investment Property Market Value

Wholesale Real Estate is real estate that is real estate priced under it's retail value. But how do you know that the retail value of real estate property? The standard formula for finding the value of real estate is to have a real estate agent find comparable (comps) properties that have sold recently. Usually about 4 properties with in a mile of the purchase property, that have sold within the past year. Formulas vary from bank to bank and real estate agent to real estate agent.

Today you can get a rough estimate by doing the research yourself. Remember that a bank will probably use their own formula, but at least you can try to get a ball park figure of a properties value by using these web sites.

Appraisal Web Sites

https://www.zillow.com/how-much-is-my-home-worth/

http://www.eppraisal.com/

12. Selecting a Real Estate Agent

So now that you have found a property, researched it's value, it's time to make an offer. Some times you have to use a government approved agent to make an offer. Like any profession, there are good agents and not so good agents.

When I lived in Virginia, once a year the local paper published a list of all the top real estate agents for almost every real estate agent franchise/business. If your local paper does not do that then here is a formula I use for selecting a real estate agent.

No part timers. Part time effort usually gets you part time results. I want an agent whose livelihood depends on their success.

Size Does Matter

The size that matters. The size or amount of properties sold. Not necessarily the gross amount of property value sold. Suppose you had a real estate agent who sold 1 million dollars worth of real estate and another who sold $500,000 worth of real estate. Which one do you choose? It depends. I want the agent who has sold the most individual properties, and not necessary the one who has the highest gross. An agent can sell only 1 house for a million dollars. The agent who sold $500,000 worth of real estate may have sold 10 $50,000 homes.

Usually a agent who makes a lot of sales has a good marketing formula in place and a good team of agents working with or for her/him. Don't be afraid to ask "who's your best agent? Why?". Often a real estate company will try to toss their worst agent a bone. Don't be that bone. Remember they work for you. Their commission comes from the property you are investing in.

Some courses teach you to negotiate the commission. I believe a proficient agent is worth the commission they desire. It's your job to select a proficient agent.

Expert Strategies to Purchase Property

13. "100-3" Formula

Here is a quick and easy formula for getting a great deal on a real estate investment property, using a real estate agent that you have build up some rapport with.

Have the agent find 100 properties for sale that have been on the market for at least 90 days. Have the agent fax an offer of 25% below market value to all of the properties. Because the properties have been on the market for at least 90 days, you are dealing with motivated sellers. It is likely that 10 out of the 100 will accept your offer. Now filter through the 10 and select the best 3 properties. Use these filters to help you select the best 3.

Strategies To Making Offers

1. What are the property taxes?

2. Are there any Homeowner Association dues?

3. What will be the appreciation value?

4. What will be your utility expenses.

5. How much will it cost, to be "live-in" ready.

6. Is it the lowest valued house in the neighboorhood?

7. What is the Crime Rate

Expert Strategies to Purchase Property

Property Taxes

I once owned two homes free and clear. The homes were in the same state. Both were similar in size, but one had a $3,000 a year property tax and the other one was $300 a year in property taxes. You can guess which one I moved first. Property taxes are often overlooked, but can be a big factor in the (TC) total cost. Do your research before you make an offer.

HOA (Home Owner Association)

Usually when a house seems like the perfect deal, but has been sitting on the market for a long time, look to see what the HOA dues are. Personally I stay away from any property that has HOA dues, because they can escalate and you have no control over them.

Appreciation

Look at the history of real estate appreciation. It can vary greatly form city to city, and neighborhood to neighborhood. If you are going for a quick flip then this is not that important.

Utility Expenses

The importance of the expense depends on what you are going to do with the property.

Expert Strategies to Purchase Property

Rehab Expenses

If you are not an expert, have a professional inspect the house so you can factor in, a accurate estimate of rehab expenses. Be aware of any possible code violations as well.

Cost relative to the Neighborhood

Usually it's easiest to sell the cheapest house in the most expensive neighborhood. However if you just plan on renting the house then this is not as big a factor.

Crime Rate

The crime rate can have a big impact on resale value. Use web sites like https://www.crimereports.com/ to help understand it's impact on your property.

14. "Take what the defense gives you"

Take what the defense gives you is a sports metaphor for viewing the landscape of a situation and adapting to what you see.

Take a similar approach to making offers in real estate. If you tell a "For Sale By Owner" everything that is wrong with the house he or she spend a lifetime building... you may insult the owner and lose the deal.

However, you send a list of needed repairs to a HUD representative, he may reduce the price of the property, no questions asked.

Adjust your offer making strategy to the person or organization you are dealing with. The farther removed a person is from the property, the less emotional they are about making deals.

Know your profit numbers and stick to them. Especially if you are bidding on a property. Be aware of Auction fever. It will bring out the competitive nature in you and can lead to you over bidding on a property. Know your numbers and be disciplined. The reason you pick out 3 properties in the 100-3 formula is so that you have 2 other properties to go to, if your first choice does not work out.

Chapter 3

Foreclosure Overview

Foreclosure Overview

What is Foreclosure

A foreclosure is when a bank, or the mortgage holder of a property takes the property of a homeowner who has not made interest and/or principal payments on time as stipulated in the mortgage contract.

Types of Foreclosure

Judicial Foreclosure

A house sold by judicial foreclosure is a mortgaged property sold by the courts. The bank or owner of the property get the proceeds, then other lien holders and even the borrower if there is anything left after the sale. Judicial foreclosures take place in all 50 states and U.S. territories.

The lender begins the process of a judicial foreclosure by filing a lawsuit against the borrower. Since it is a legal action, everyone involved must be notified of the proceedings. Notification of the proceedings can vary from state to state(classified ads to posted notices). There is usually a hearing to determine the proceedings.

Foreclosure Overview

Nonjudicial Foreclosure

Some jurisdictions allow lenders to foreclose property without getting a court order first (a power of sale clause). This is called a non-judicial foreclosure.

Non-judicial foreclosure is only available for deeds of trust with power-of-sale clauses. They are not available for traditional mortgages.

Where available, non-judicial foreclosures are heavily regulated. Generally, before foreclosing, lenders must give special notice to the property-owner. Afterwards, lenders must wait a specified time before auctioning off the property.

Strict Foreclosures

Strict foreclosure is only available in a few states like Connecticut, New Hampshire and Vermont. If a mortgagee wins a court case, the court orders the defaulted mortgagor to pay the mortgage within a specified period of time. Should the mortgagor fail to do so, the mortgage holder gains the title to the property with no obligation to sell it. This type of foreclosure is generally available only when the value of the property is less than the debt.

Foreclosure Overview

Real Estate Investor Overview

Start-up Cost: $10,000 - $50,000

Potential Earnings: $25,000 - Unlimited

Typical Fees: No money down to
                                  unlimited

Advertising: Real Estate Publications.
Real Estate Agents. Social media.

Qualifications: Knowledge of the real
estate market. Access to Capital. Maintenance
                                  Knowledge.

Equipment Needed: Cell phone. Computer.
Internet access. Home repair tools.

Foreclosure Overview

Home Business Potential: Yes

Staff Required: Yes & No.

Hidden Cost: Appraisals, interest,
finance fees, eviction costs, downturns in the real
estate market.

Now lets take a closer look at each one of these real
estate investor requirements.

Start up costs

Recently I purchased a 5 bedroom home with over
half an acre back yard for under $7,000 from a bank.
So you can litterally start your business with 1 or 2
credit cards if you have no money at all.

In another chapter in this book you will be shown
how to find real estate at a deep discount on a
consistant basis. Many people simply don't believe
they can purchase property for the price of a
automobile. They have been culturally programmed
to start out with an apartment, then go to a real
estate agent to purchase a home. That is one reason
there are so many low cost homes available. A
recession and the economy in general is another.
What ever the reason, great deals are almost
everywhere.

Foreclosure Overview

Potential Earnings

I have made tens of thousands of dollars flipping property and renting property out for hundreds of dollars of monthly positive cash flow. Both have their advantages. Either way your potential earnings are limitless. The most important thing is to understand total cost.

Total Cost is the total amount of money expended to establish an investment position. Total cost includes commissions, accrued interest, and taxes, in addition to the principal amount of securities traded. Anticipate all costs, **before** you invest in a property.

Advertising

Real estate magazines and online classified ads like craigslist are a great place to advertise a home for sale or rent. However, Social Media has become more and more relevant in the real estate investing business. There are all types of social media web sites. Pinterest, Facebook, Instagram and Twitter to name a fee. However for real estate investing I believe there is no substitute for YouTube. From the comfort of their home, a person can take a complete walk through your property. YouTube is free and reatively easy to get started.

Foreclosure Overview

Qualifications: Knowledge of the Market

A man's machine broke. He spent hours, then days trying to fix it. Finally he called a professional repair man. In just a few seconds, the repair man pulled out a hammer, whacked the machine and it was fixed. The man was handed a bill of $100. The man said "I'm not paying you $100 for just swinging your hammer." The repair man responded "you are not paying a $100 to me for swinging my hammer. You are paying a $100 to me for knowing where and how to swing my hammer."

Success in real estate investing is not complicated. Buy low. Sell higher. You simply need to know, what is low and how to find it. There is no substitute for patience and research. When I purchased that home from the bank for $7,000, I had been going online for 3 hours a day for months, viewing properties from multiple real estate web sites.

Viewing so many homes, gave me a masterful knowledge of the market, so I could then easily determine what is low and what is high in the market. It also gave me an idea of how long it took for properties to sell and for how much. Every market is different. Don't take a real estate agent's word for things. Make their word part of determining the market for yourself.

Foreclosure Overview

Equipment Needed

Today you need a cell phone, a computer and a good internet connection to be an effective real estate investor. When you are starting out, it may also help if you have an ability to do some property repairs yourself.

Places like Home Depot and Lowes offer free classes on many typical home repairs. If you are going to do repairs yourself, then you will also need to add home repair tools, like a circular saw, a hammer, wrenches and drills, to the list of "equipment needed".

Staff Required

Do you need a staff? Yes and no. No, because you don't have to have people on payroll. Yes because you are going to need assistance to run this business effectively.

Your team should include but not be limited to, a real estate attorney, several quality real estate agents, at least 2 handymen, and a bank loan officer or private money lender.

Foreclosure Overview

Hidden Costs

Attorney fees, Appraisals, interest, finance fees, eviction costs, downturns in the real estate market. Are just a few of the hidden costs in real estate investing.

When hiring an attorney, make sure you find one that specializes in real estate investing. One who knows contracts inside and out. Making this quality investment will help to reduce the cost on the majority of the other hidden fees.

CHAPTER 4

REAL ESTATE FINANCING 4,000 Sources!

8 Realistic Ways to Finance Real Estate

FINANCING REAL ESTATE

Welcome to Expert financing. I am going to show you several realistic ways to finance real estate. You are going to learn how to finance real estate with.

* VA LOANS

* PARTNERS

* INVESTMENT CLUBS

* CREDIT CARDS

* CORPORATE CREDIT

* EQUITY

* SELLER FINANCE

* HARD MONEY LENDERS

* AND FINALLY I SHOW YOU THE MONEY$!!

USING A VA LOAN

According to the web sites www.benefits.va.gov and www.military.com the current VA Loan amount is a whopping $417,000! What a lot of veterans don't know is that you can use that money to purchase not only your home, but investment properties. That is how I started my investing career. Purchasing multiple homes using my VA Loan.

FINANCING REAL ESTATE

Even if you are not a veteran, you can still partner up with one, who still has some money left on his or her VA LOAN.

If you are a Veteran, you will need to obtain a copy of your DD 214 and VA Form 26-1880 Request for a Certificate of Eligibility.

PARTNERS

This is another way I purchased a home. At the time I worked for the United States Postal Service. I had already purchased plenty of homes, so many of the workers were aware I had successfully invested in real estate. At break time I went around and ask people to partner up with me. I had multiple people offer to go in as a partner. I choose one and that house we rehabbed and flipped just two months after purchasing it. To this day it was the biggest gross profit on one deal, I have had. True I had to split it with my partner, but I would rather have half of something than all of nothing.

Having the combined resources of two people can be a great benefit, but it is not without it's challenges. If you are going to use a partner, no matter how close you are...GET EVERY THING IN WRITING.

FINANCING REAL ESTATE

Having a partner can dramatically increase the chance of a Bank lending money as well as having someone to split the work on rehabbing, should you decide to save money and make repairs yourself. But all this must be spelled out BEFORE you enter into a Agreement/Contract and purchase a home.

It helps if the person is like minded and understands the risks and benefits of investing, and truly understands the return on investment of a particular deal.

REAL ESTATE INVESTMENT CLUBS

Real estate investment clubs are groups that meet locally and allow investors and other professionals to network and learn. They can provide extremely useful information for both the novice and expert real estate investor. A top real estate club can provide a great forum to network, learn about reputable contractors, brokers, realtors, lawyers, accountants and other professionals. On the other hand, there are many real estate clubs designed to sell you. They bring in "gurus" who sell either on stage or at the back of the room, and as a result, the clubs typically profit to the tune of %50 of the sale price of the product, bootcamp, or training that is pitched.

FINANCING REAL ESTATE

I have purchased a ton of real estate books and real estate courses. Carlton Sheets, Dave Del Dotto, The Mylands, Seminar courses and much much more. I am not against any club bringing in a speaker who has a course. However I think there should be transparency to the members of the club.

There is certainly value in the networking that may come at one of these groups. But attend working to attain your goals and not necessarily the club's goal to sell you something. Some times both are the same thing. As a rule I usually leave debit cards at home the first time I attend an event. If there is a seller there with a "This day only offer" then I won't feel pressured to purchase. Plus most sellers can be convinced to sell at the discount offer price at a later time when you have had a chance to come down off the "sense of urgency emotional pitch" .

CREDIT CARDS

When using a credit card in real estate you must really do your homework on the deal. Dan Kennedy a world famous marketer once said "always stack the numbers in your favor". That's how you use a credit card. Look at the return on investment as compared to the long term cost of using a credit card and it's interest. Also I would recommend buying low cost homes that you can purchase and own free and clear.

FINANCING REAL ESTATE

No Mortgage Payment!!! My last 2 homes I have purchased have been cash deals. One home cost $1,500 and the other about $7,000. The first was a government property from HUD and the 2nd From a Bank. These institutions are unemotional about real estate and simply view a property as a non performing asset. The 2nd home was 4 bedrooms, 1 1/2 bath and a basement located in a farming community and came with a 2 car garage/shed and   .6 acre(that is the size of a NFL football field) of land.

In this book I show you how to find plenty of houses with amazing below wholesale prices and a formula for almost always finding a great deal.

CORPORATE CREDIT

Many people set up corporations to buy and sell real estate as an additional protection against liabilities. Other's create a corporation to mask personal involvement in property transfers and public records. Regardless of the use of a corporation, you can buy real estate with corporate credit as an alternative to using your own cash or IRA. By capitalizing on the credit rating of your corporation, you can buy real estate and build your corporate holdings portfolio.

FINANCING REAL ESTATE

Just remember that you can set up your corporation in a state that favors you the most for your real estate deals. Do your research. Most people like Delaware and Nevada, but you will have to decide if your home state or any other state is best for you and your business.

CURRENT EQUITY

Using the equity in your home for real estate investing is another way you can finance properties. You might use the money for a down payment or it may only be enough to cover the cost of some rehab repairs.

If you stick to the low cost home formula, you may have enough to purchase the entire house. A house is an investment that should appreciate in value as well as give a great ROI (Return On Investment). When you decide to flip the property or rent it out for positive cashflow.

If you have equity and it's not doing anything, then you may decide to make it a "performing asset" and use it as part of your real estate finance program.

FINANCING REAL ESTATE

SELLER FINANCING

Seller finance is where the seller of a free and clear property becomes your bank along with being the seller.

Advantages:

You get to purchase the property on terms that may be more beneficial for you. Seller gets monthly payments and the benefit of treating the sale as an installment sale thus allowing them to defer any capital gains taxes that may be due.

Disadvantages:

You may be locked into a mortgage with a pre-payment penalty or may not be able to resell the property immediately. This strategy is typically not meant for flipping but can definitely be used for that purpose if structured correctly.

Seller Finance is a known way to finance a property. That is why I have presented it in this book. But it is my least favorite because you now have a lingering relationship with your property. Your ability to make decisions regarding the property is limited and for that reason, I would not go this route. However, like all types of financing, you have to ask yourself, "is the deal worth it."

FINANCING REAL ESTATE

I also prefer to work alone, but when a great deal came along, I sought out a partner to make it happen. Risk is usually relative to potential profit.

HARD MONEY LENDERS

A hard money lender is usually a individual or company that lends money for an investment secured by the investment property.

Advantages:

Less red tape to get the money. You are dealing with people who understand the real estate investment business.

Disadvantage:

This is not a long term loan. The lender wants a return on investment, usually within a few months, a a year, or a few years. The interest rate on the loan is much higher than usual conventional banks.

Using hard money has a higher risk because the return on investment is due quicker. Therefore it is a good idea not to use a Hard Money Lender, until you have a great deal of experience and confidence in being able to produce a return on investment.

SHOWING YOU THE MONEY

A list of web sites for financing.

www.businessfinance.com (4,000 sources of money!)

www.advanceamericaproperty.com

http://www.cashadvanceloan.com/

www.brookviewfinancial.com

www.commercialfundingcorp.com

www.dhlc.com
(hard money for the Texas area)

www.equity-funding.com

www.bankofamerica.com

www.carolinahardmoney.com
(for real estate investors in North and South
Carolina)

www.fpfloans.com

FINANCING REAL ESTATE

As you can see there are plenty of strategies for financing a property. Do your research on your investment property and get the true market value. Purchase well below wholesale. This will help to minimize risk and elevate your potential profit margins. Buying below wholesale also creates a buffer for unexpected expenses.

So don't let the lack of money be a roadblock in your real estate investing dreams.

Chapter 5

Texas
Cash Flow
Counties
of
Wholesale
Property!

Texas Cash Flow Counties of Wholesale Property!

The internet has made it possible to grow your real estate investing business quickly and easily. Now you can view hundreds of properties online without ever leaving your home.

In this chapter I am going to give you a ton of web sites and the addresses to government wholesale sources, to help you to cover this state's real estate goldmines. I have selected some of the biggest counties with the largest supply of wholesale real estate.

In general you should look at 100 homes for every 1 property that you purchase. Comparing factors like the home value, rent potential, repair cost, local taxes, possible home owner fees, utilities etc...

While there is no substitute for inspecting a home in person, having access to thousands of homes on the internet can help you to narrow down the field to spectacular deals! So take advantage of this knowledge to help secure your real estate investing success!

Texas Cash Flow Counties of Wholesale Property!

Locate Statewide Texas Properties

MLS.com

http://www.mls.com/search/Texas.mvc

Texas Real Estate Foreclosures with links to different cities on the landing page.

REALTOR.com

http://www.realtor.com/foreclosures/Texas

Links to Texas real estate properties by county and city.

Top Texas Counties

The previous web sites give you access to a broad selection of property in all the counties in Texas.

Next I narrow it down to a handful of the top counties based on the population size, rising property values, rental profit potential and the abundance of wholesale property available.

Texas Cash Flow Counties of Wholesale Property!

1. Harris County

Harris County has a population of 4,092,459 and is 1,729 square miles.

Tax Property Info Street Address:

Harris County Tax Office
1001 Preston St., Houston, TX 77002
Phone: (713) 274-8000

Tax sale questions and answers:

http://taxsales.lgbs.com/faqs?state=texas

Foreclosures web Address:

https://urlzs.com/JAD4p

Tax Sales web site:

https://www.hctax.net/Property/TaxSales/TaxSales

Texas Cash Flow Counties of Wholesale Property!

2. Dallas County

Dallas County has a population of 2,368,139 and is 880 square miles.

Tax Property Info Street Address:

City of Garland Tax Office
217 North Fifth St., Garland, TX 75040
Phone (972)205-2410 Fax (972)205-3834

Foreclosures web Address:

https://urlzs.com/BjCNQ

Tax Sales web site:

https://www.pbfcm.com/taxresale.html

Texas Cash Flow Counties of Wholesale Property!

3. Tarrant County

Tarrant County has a population of 1,809,537 and is 864 square miles.

Tax Property Info Street Address:

Tarrant County Tax Assessor and Collector
100 East Weatherford St., Fort Worth, TX 76196
Phone (817)884-1100

Foreclosures web Address:

https://urlzs.com/8feiP

Tax Sales web site:

https://urlzs.com/McQwg

Texas Cash Flow Counties of Wholesale Property!

4. Bexar County

Bexar County has a population of 1,714,773 and is 1,247 square miles.

Tax Property Info Street Address:

Bexar County Tax Assessor and Collector
Vista Verde Plaza Building
233 North Pecos La Trinidad, San Antonio, TX 78207
Phone (210)335-2251

Foreclosures web Address:

https://maps.bexar.org/foreclosures/

Tax Sales web site:

https://www.pbfcm.com/taxresale.html

Texas Cash Flow Counties of Wholesale Property!

5. Travis County

Travis County has a population of 1,024,266 and is 989 square miles.

Tax Property Info Street Address:

Travis County Tax Assessor and Collector
5501 Airport Blvd., Austin, TX 78751
Phone (512)854-9473 Fax (512)854-9056

Foreclosures web Address:

https://tax-office.traviscountytx.gov/foreclosure

Tax Sales web site:

https://tax-office.traviscountytx.gov/foreclosure

6. El Paso County

El Paso County has a population of 782,341 and is 848 square miles.

Tax Property Info Street Address:

El Paso County Tax Assessor and Collector
301 Manny Martinez Dr., El Paso, TX 79905
Phone (915) 771-2300 Fax (915) 771-2301

Foreclosures web Address:

http://epcounty.com/sheriff/cp_saleinfo.htm

Tax Sales web site:

https://www.pbfcm.com/taxresale.html

Texas Cash Flow Counties of Wholesale Property!

7. Hidalgo County

Hidalgo County has a population of 774,769 and is 1,569 square miles.

Tax Property Info Street Address:

Hidalgo County Tax Assessor and Collector
Hidalgo County Administration Bldg
2804 S US Hwy 281, Edinburg, TX 78539
Phone (956)318-2157

Foreclosures web Address:

https://urlzs.com/akp3N

Tax Sales web site:

https://www.pbfcm.com/taxresale.html

Chapter 6

Texas
Real Estate
Investing
City Goldmines

Texas Real Estate Investing

City Goldmines

1. Houston

The city of Houston has a population of 2,267,336 to support your real estate investing business.

The median home value in Houston is $186,000. Houston is a real estate goldmine city because recently the home values have gone up 5.4 percent and is expected to rise at least another 1.9 percent.

Houses currently listed in Houston have a median price of about $300,000.

The median rent price in Houston is about $1,525. This ranks #5 between Texas Goldmine Cities.

Foreclosure Warning sign

Delinquent mortgages in Houston is 1.2 percent. The *Foreclosure potiential rank is #6 between Texas goldmine cities.*

Texas Real Estate Investing

City Goldmines

2. San Antonio

The city of San Antonio has a population of 1,461,623 to support your real estate investing business.

The median home value in San Antonio is $176,100. San Antonio is a real estate goldmine city because recently the home values have gone up 5.9 percent and is expected to rise at least another 2.4 percent.

Houses currently listed in San Antonio have a median price of about $245,000.

The median rent price in San Antonio is about $1,299. This ranks #6 between Texas Goldmine Cities.

Foreclosure Warning sign

Delinquent mortgages in San Antonio is 1.6 percent. The *Foreclosure potiential rank is #1 between Texas goldmine cities.*

3. Dallas

The city of Dallas has a population of 1,300,122 to support your real estate investing business.

The median home value in Dallas is $214,000. Dallas is a real estate goldmine city because recently the home values have gone up 14.2 percent and is expected to rise at least another 7.5 percent.

Houses currently listed in Dallas have a median price of about $399,900.

The median rent price in Dallas is about $1,705. This ranks #1 between Texas Goldmine Cities.

Foreclosure Warning sign

Delinquent mortgages in Dallas is 1.3 percent. The Foreclosure potiential rank is #5 between Texas goldmine cities.

Texas Real Estate Investing

City Goldmines

4. Austin

The city of Austin has a population of 916,906 to support your real estate investing business.

The median home value in Austin is $368,600. Austin is a real estate goldmine city because recently the home values have gone up 6.5 percent and is expected to rise at least another 3.4 percent.

Houses currently listed in Austin have a median price of about $400,000.

The median rent price in Austin is about $1,700. This ranks #2 between Texas Goldmine Cities.

Foreclosure Warning sign

Delinquent mortgages in Austin is .4 percent. The *Foreclosure potiential rank is #7 between Texas goldmine cities.*

5. Fort Worth

The city of Fort Worth has a population of 835,129 to support your real estate investing business.

The median home value in Fort Worth is $197,400. Fort Worth is a real estate goldmine city because recently the home values have gone up 8.5 percent and is expected to rise at least another 4.3 percent.

Houses currently listed in Fort Worth have a median price of about $262,990.

The median rent price in Fort Worth is about $1,625. This ranks #3 between Texas Goldmine Cities.

Foreclosure Warning sign

Delinquent mortgages in Fort Worth is 1.5 percent. The Foreclosure potiential rank is #3 between Texas goldmine cities.

Texas Real Estate Investing

City Goldmines

6. El Paso

The city of El Paso has a population of 678,266 to support your real estate investing business.

The median home value in El Paso is $128,800. El Paso is a real estate goldmine city because recently the home values have gone up 5.0 percent.

Houses currently listed in El Paso have a median price of about $184,950.

The median rent price in El Paso is about $1,150. This ranks #7 between Texas Goldmine Cities.

Foreclosure Warning sign

Delinquent mortgages in El Paso is 1.6 percent. The Foreclosure potiential rank is #1 between Texas goldmine cities.

7. Arlington

The city of Arlington has a population of 388,225 to support your real estate investing business.

The median home value in Arlington is $207,900. Arlington is a real estate goldmine city because recently the home values have gone up 8.3 percent and is expected to rise at least another 4.0 percent.

Houses currently listed in Arlington have a median price of about $249,950.

The median rent price in Arlington is about $1,600. This ranks #4 between Texas Goldmine Cities.

Foreclosure Warning sign

Delinquent mortgages in Arlington is 1.4 percent. The *Foreclosure potiential rank is #4 between Texas goldmine cities.*

Chapter 7

Zero Cost Business Launch Formula

ZERO COST MARKETING

While there are many ways to market we are only going focuse on ZERO COST MARKETING. You are starting up. You can always go for the more expensive ways of marketing after your business is producing income.

FREE WEB HOSTING

Get a free web site. You can get a free web site at weebly.com or wix.com. Or just type "free web hosting" in a google, bing or yahoo search engine.

Free web hosting is something you can use for a varitey or reasons. However many free web hosting sites add an extention to the name of your web address that lets everyone know you are using their services. For this reason you eventually want to scale up once you start making income.

LOW COST PAID WEB HOSTING

Free is nice, but you when you need to expand your business it is best to go with a paid web hosting service. There are several that give you good value for under $10.00 a month.

1. Yahoo small business

2. Intuit.com

3. ipage.com

4. Hostgator.com

5. Godaddy.com

Yahoo small business allows for unlimited web pages and is probably the best overall value, but they require a years payment up front. Intuit allows for monthly payments.

For free ecommerce on your web site, open up a Paypal account and get the HTML code for payment buttons for free. Then put those buttons on your web site.

Step by Step basic zero cost web site traffic instructions

Step 1 zero cost internet marketing

Now that your web site is up and running you should register it with at least the top 3 search engines. 1. Google 2. Bing 3. Yahoo.

Step 2 zero cost internet marketing

Write and submit a **press release**. Google "free press release sites" for press release sites that will allow you to summit press releases for free. If you do not know how to write a press release go to www.fiverr.com and sub-contract the work out for only $5.00 !!!

Step 3 zero cost internet marketing

Write and submit articles to article marketing web sites like **ezinearticles.com.**

Step 4 zero cost internet marketing

Create and submit videos to video sharing sites like dailymotion.com or **youtube.com.** Make sure to include a hyperlink to your website in the description of your videos.

Step 5 zero cost internet marketing

Submit your web site to **dmoz.org**. This is a huge open directory that many smaller search engines go to get web sites for their database.

ZERO COST MARKETING

In an interview with Tom Bilyeu Multi-millionaire Rahel Hollis, the author of "Girl wash your face" , said that every thing she that taught her how to build her multi-million dollar empire, she learned from watching free YouTube videos.

You can start a successful business without spending a bunch of money. You just have to gain the proper knowledge and be willing to do "what ever it takes" to succeed!

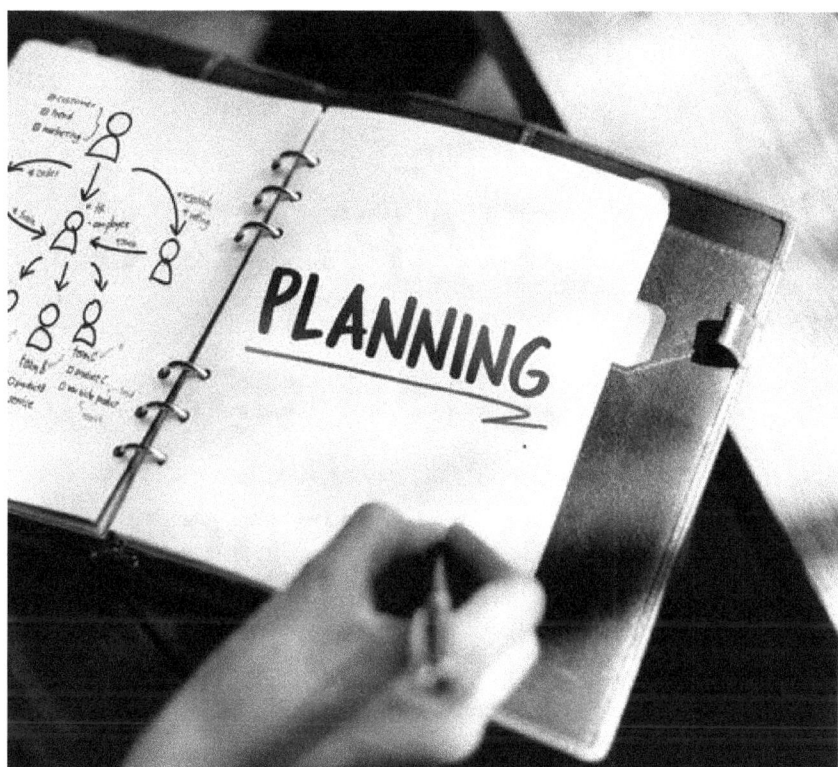

CHAPTER 8
Business
Insurance

BUSINESS INSURANCE

Consult an attorney for any and all of your business matters.

In the early 1990's an elderly woman purchased a hot cup of coffee from a McDonald's drive-thru window in Albuquerque. She spilled the coffee, and suffered 3rd degree burns. She sued Mcdonald's and won. She won 2.7 million dollars in a punitive damages victory. The verdict was appealed and settlement is estimated at somewhere in the neighborhood of $500,000 dollars. All because she spilled the coffee into her lap, while trying to add sugar and cream.

Two men in Ohio, were carpet layers. They were severely burned when a three and a half gallon container of carpet adhesive ignited, when the hot water heater it was sitting next to, was turned on. They felt the warning lable on the back of the can was insufficient. So they filed a lawsuit against the adhesive manufacturers and were awarded nine million dollars.

A woman in Oklahoma, purchased a brand new Winnebago. While driving it home, she set the cruise control to 70 miles per hour. She then left the drivers seat to make some coffee or a sandwich in the back of the motor home.

BUSINESS INSURANCE

The vehicle crashed and the woman sued Winnebago for not advising her, that cruise control does not drive and steer the vehicle. She won 1.7 million dollars and the company had to rewrite their instruction manual.

Unfortunately all three outrageous lawsuits are real. If you are going to run a business, any business, you should consider protecting yourself with Professional Liability Insurance, also known as Errors and Omissions (E & 0) insurance.

This type of insurance can help to protect you from having to pay the full cost of defending yourself against a negligence lawsuit claim.

Error and Omissions can protect you against claims that are not usually covered in regular liability insurance. Those policies usually cover bodily harm, or damage to property. Error and Omissions can protect you agaist negligence, and other mental anguish like inaccurate advice, or misrepresentation. Criminal prosecution is not covered.

Errors and Ommision insurance is recommended for notaries public, real estate brokers or investors and professionals like: software engineers, lawyers, home inspectors web site delvelopers and landscape architects to name a few professions.

BUSINESS INSURANCE

The Most Common Errors and Omission Claims:

%25 Breach of Fiduciary Duty

%15 Breach of Contract

%14 Negligence

%13 Failure to Supervise

%11 Unsuitability

%10 Other

BUSINESS INSURANCE

Things you should know about or require before purchasing a Errors and Omission policy is...

* What is the limit of liability

* What is the Deductible

* Does it include FDD First Dollar Defense - which obligates the insurance company to fight a case without a deductible first.

* Do I have Tail-end coverage or Extended Reporting Coverage (insurance that lasts into retirement)

* Extended coverage for Employees

* Cyber Liability Coverage

* Department of Labor Fiduciary Coverage

* Insolvency Coverage

If you get Errors and Omission insurance, renew it the day it expires. You must be careful to avoid gaps in your coverage, or it could result in not getting your policy renewed.

BUSINESS INSURANCE

A few E & O Insurance Providers:

Insureon

Insureon states that their median Errors and Omissions Insurance policy cost about $750 a year or about $65 a month. The price of course will vary according to your business, the policy you choose and other risk factors.

https://www.insureon.com/home

EOforless

EOforless.com helps insurance, investment, and real estate professionals buy E & O insurance at an affordable cost in five minutes or less.

https://www.eoforless.com/

BUSINESS INSURANCE

CalSurance Associates

As a leading insurance broker, CalSurance Associates, a division of Brown & Brown Program Insurance Services, Inc. has over fifty years of experience delivering comprehensive insurance products, exceptional service, and proven results to over 150,000 insured. They provide professionals nationwide and across multiple industries, including some of the largest financial firms and insurance companies in the United States.

http://www.calsurance.com/csweb/index.aspx

Better Safe Than Sorry

Insurance is one of the hidden costs of doing business. These are just a few companies and a brief overview on the topic of business insurance. Make sure to talk to an attorney or quailified insurance agent before making any decision on insurance. Protect you and your business. Many states do not require E & O insurances. But when you see the cost of some of the settlements, it's better to be safe than sorry.

Chapter 9

Getting Started in Business

Step by Step

Getting Started in Business

There are over thirty million home-based businesses in the United States alone.

Many people dream of the independence and financial reward of having a home business. Unfortunately they let analysis paralysis stop them from taking action. This chapter is designed to give you a road map to get started. The most difficult step in any journey is the first step.

Anthony Robbins created a program called Personal Power. I studied the program a long time ago, and today I would summarize it, by saying you must figure out a way to motivate yourself to take massive action without fear of failure.

2 Timothy 1:7 King James Version

"For God hath not given us the spirit of fear; but of power, and of love, and of a sound mind."

STEP #1 MAKE AN OFFICE IN YOUR HOUSE

If you are serious about making money, then redo the man cave or the woman's cave and make a place for you to do business, uninterupted.

STEP #2 BUDGET OUT TIME FOR YOUR BUSINESS

If you already have a job, or if you have children, then they can take up a great deal of your time. Not to mention well meaning friends who use the phone to become time theives. Budget time for your business and stick to it.

STEP #3 DECIDE ON THE TYPE OF BUSINESS

You don't have to be rigid, but begin with the end in mine. You can become more flexible as you gain experience.

STEP #4 LEGAL FORM FOR YOUR BUSINESS

The three basic legal forms are sole proprietorship, partnership, and corporation. Each one has it's advantages. Go to www.Sba.gov and learn about each and make a decision.

STEP #5 PICK A BUSINESS NAME AND REGISTER IT

One of the safest ways to pick a business name is to use your own name. By using your own name you don't have to worry about copy right violations.

However, always check with an Attorney or the proper legal authority when dealing with legal matters.

STEP #6 WRITE A BUSINESS PLAN

This would seem like a no brainer. No matter what you are trying to accomplish you should have a blueprint. You should have a business plan. In the NFL about seven headcoaches get fired every season. So in a very competetive business, a man with no head coaching experience got hired by the NFL's Philadelphia Eagles. His name was Andy Reid. Andy Reid would later become the most successful coach in the team's history. One of the reasons the owner hired him, was because he had a business plan the size of a telephone book. Your business plan does not need to be nearly that big, but if you plan for as much as possible, you are less likely to get rattled when things don't go as planned.

STEP #7 PROPER LICENSES & PERMITS

Go to city hall and find out what you need to do, to start a home business.

STEP #8 PUT UP A WEB SITE, SELECT BUSINESS CARDS, STATIONERY, BROCHURES

This is one of the least expensive ways to not only start your business but to promote and network your business.

STEP #9 OPEN A BUSINESS CHECKING ACCOUNT

Having a separate business account makes it much easier to keep track of profit and expenses. This will come in handy, whether you decide to do your own taxes or hire out an professional.

STEP #10 TAKE SOME SORT OF ACTION TODAY!

This is not meant to be a comprehensive plan to start a business. It is meant to point you in the right direction to get started. You can go to the Small Business Administration for many free resources for starting your business. They even have a program(SCORE) that will give you access to many retired professionals who will advise you for free! Their web site: **www.score.org**

Chapter 10

REAL ESTATE
DEFINITIONS

Real Estate Definitions

Acceleration Clause - A contract provision that allows a lender to require a borrower to repay all or part of an outstanding loan if certain requirements are not met. An acceleration clause outlines the reasons that the lender can demand loan repayment. Also known as "acceleration covenant".

Active Income - Active income is income for which services have been performed. This includes wages, tips, salaries, commissions and income from businesses in which there is material participation.

Agent - One who is legally authorized to act on behalf of another person.

All-inclusive deed of trust (AITD) - An All Inclusive Trust Deed (AITD) is a new deed of trust that includes the balance due on the existing note plus new funds advanced; also known as a wrap-around mortgage.

Amortized loan - An amortized loan is a loan with scheduled periodic payments that consist of both principal and interest. An amortized loan payment pays the relevant interest expense for the period before any principal is paid and reduced.

Real Estate Definitions

Appraiser - A practitioner who has the knowledge and expertise necessary to estimate the value of an asset, or the likelihood of an event occurring, and the cost of such an occurrence.

Asking price - the price at which something is offered for sale.

Assignment - An assignment (Latin cessio) is a term used with similar meanings in the law of contracts and in the law of real estate. In both instances, it encompasses the transfer of rights held by one party—the assignor—to another party—the assignee.

At-risk rule - Tax laws limiting the amount of losses an investor (usually a limited partner) can claim. Only the amount actually at risk can be deducted.

Balloon mortgage - a mortgage in which a large portion of the borrowed principal is repaid in a single payment at the end of the loan period.

Capital gain - a profit from the sale of property or of an investment.

Cash flow - the total amount of money being transferred into and out of a business, especially as affecting liquidity.

Real Estate Definitions

Chattel - an item of property other than real estate.

Co-insurance - a type of insurance in which the insured pays a share of the payment made against a claim.

Contract of sale - A real estate contract is a contract between parties for the purchase and sale, exchange, or other conveyance of real estate.

Declining balance method - A declining balance method is a common depreciation-calculation system that involves applying the depreciation rate against the non-depreciated balance.

Depreciation - Depreciation is an accounting method of allocating the cost of a tangible asset over its useful life. Businesses depreciate long-term assets for both tax and accounting purposes.

Earnest money - Earnest money is a deposit made to a seller showing the buyer's good faith in a transaction. Often used in real estate transactions, earnest money allows the buyer additional time when seeking financing. Earnest money is typically held jointly by the seller and buyer in a trust or escrow account.

Real Estate Definitions

Equity participation - Equity participation is the ownership of shares in a company or property. ... The greater the equity participation rate, the higher the percentage of shares owned by stakeholders. Allowing stakeholders to own shares ties the stakeholders' success with that of the company or real estate investment.

Estoppel - Estoppel Certificate. An estoppel certificate is a document used in mortgage negotiations to establish facts and financial obligations, such as outstanding amounts due that can affect the settlement of a loan. It is required by a lender of a third party in a real estate transaction.

Fee simple - In English law, a fee simple or fee simple absolute is an estate in land, a form of freehold ownership. It is a way that real estate may be owned in common law countries, and is the highest possible ownership interest that can be held in real property.

Gift deed - Quitclaim Deed Vs. Gift Deed. Property deeds define and protect ownership in a home. In real estate, deeds are legal documents that transfer ownership of a property from one party to another. ... Each type of deed is used for a specific situation.

Real Estate Definitions

Gross income - A real estate investment term, Gross Operating Income refers to the result of subtracting the credit and vacancy losses from a property's gross potential income. Also Known As: Effective Gross Income (EGI)

Income approach to value - The income approach is a real estate appraisal method that allows investors to estimate the value of a property by taking the net operating income of the rent collected and dividing it by the capitalization rate.

Interest - Estates and ownership interests defined. The law recognizes different sorts of interests, called estates, in real property. The type of estate is generally determined by the language of the deed, lease, bill of sale, will, land grant, etc., through which the estate was acquired.

Joint and several note - Joint and several note is a promissory note which is the note of all and of each of the makers as to its legal obligation between the parties to it.

Real Estate Definitions

Lease option - A lease option (more formally Lease With the Option to Purchase) is a type of contract used in both residential and commercial real estate. In a lease-option, a property owner and tenant agree that, at the end of a specified rental period for a given property, the renter has the option of purchasing the property.

Like kind property - Like-Kind Property. Any two assets or properties that are considered to be the same type, making an exchange between them tax free. To qualify as like kind, two assets must be of the same type (e.g. two pieces of residential real estate), but do not have to be of the same quality.

Loan to value - The loan to value or LTV ratio of a property is the percentage of the property's value that is mortgaged. ... Loan to Value is used in commercial real estate as well. Examples: $300,000 appraised value of a home. $240,000 mortgage on the property. $240,000 / $300,000 = .80 or 80% Loan to Value Ratio

Mortgage broker - A mortgage broker is an intermediary working with a borrower and a lender while qualifying the borrower for a mortgage. The broker gathers income, asset and employment documentation, a credit report and other information for assessing the borrower's ability to secure financing.

Real Estate Definitions

Net rentable area - Actual square-unit of a building that may be leased or rented to tenants, the area upon which the lease or rental payments are computed. It usually excludes common areas, elevator shafts, stairways, and space devoted to cooling, heating, or other equipment. Also called net leasable area.

Option - A real estate purchase option is a contract on a specific piece of real estate that allows the buyer the exclusive right to purchase the property. Once a buyer has an option to buy a property, the seller cannot sell the property to anyone else.

Possession - A principle of real estate law that allows a person who possesses someone else's land for an extended period of time to claim legal title to that land.

Prepayment penalty - Prepayment Penalty. A prepayment penalty is a clause in a mortgage contract stating that a penalty will be assessed if the mortgage is prepaid within a certain time period. The penalty is based on a percentage of the remaining mortgage balance or a certain number of months' worth of interest.

Real Estate Definitions

Promissory note - In the United States, a mortgage note (also known as a real estate lien note, borrower's note) is a promissory note secured by a specified mortgage loan; it is a written promise to repay a specified sum of money plus interest at a specified rate and length of time to fulfill the promise.

Real estate owned (REO) - Real estate owned or REO is a term used in the United States to describe a class of property owned by a lender—typically a bank, government agency, or government loan insurer—after an unsuccessful sale at a foreclosure auction.

Refinancing - Getting a new mortgage to replace the original is called refinancing. Refinancing is done to allow a borrower to obtain a better interest term and rate. The first loan is paid off, allowing the second loan to be created, instead of simply making a new mortgage and throwing out the original mortgage.

Reproduction cost - The costs involved with identically reproducing an asset or property with the same materials and specifications as an insured property based on current prices.

Real Estate Definitions

Right of survivorship - The right of survivorship is an attribute of several types of joint ownership of property, most notably joint tenancy and tenancy in common. When jointly owned property includes a right of survivorship, the surviving owner automatically absorbs a dying owner's share of the property. Thus if A and B jointly own a house with a right of survivorship, and B dies, A becomes the sole owner of the house, despite any contrary intent in B's will.

Standby commitment - A standby commitment is a formal agreement by a bank agreeing to lend money to a borrower up to a specified amount for a specific period. It is also known as firm commitment lending. The amount given under standby commitment is to be used only in specified contingency.

Supply and demand - The law of supply and demand is a basic economic principle that explains the relationship between supply and demand for a good or service and how the interaction affects the price of that good or service. The relationship of supply and demand affects the housing market and the price of a house

Real Estate Definitions

Tenancy by entirety - Tenants by entirety (TBE) is a method in some states by which married couples can hold the title to a property. In order for one spouse to modify his or her interest in the property in any way, the consent of both spouses is required by tenants by entirety.

Title insurance policy - Title insurance is an insurance policy that covers the loss of ownership interest in a property due to legal defects and is required if the property is under mortgage. The most common type of title insurance is a lender's title insurance, which is paid for by the borrower but protects only the lender.

Vacancy and rent loss - Vacancy and Credit Loss in real estate investing is the amount of money or percentage of net operating income that is estimated to not be realized due to non-payment of rents and vacant units

Will - A will or testament is a legal document by which a person, the testator, expresses their wishes as to how their property is to be distributed at death, and names one or more persons, the executor, to manage the estate until its final distribution.

$10,000 MegaSized Internet Marketing & Copy Writing & SEO Course & $1,000 Value Bonus

LIBRARY I (Video Training Programs)

1. Product Creation
2. Copy Writing & Payment
3. Auto Responder & Product Download Page
4. How to start a Freelancing business
5. Video Marketing
6. List Building
7. Affiliate Marketing
8. How to Get Massive Web Site Traffic

LIBRARY II (Video Training Programs)

1. Goldmine Government Grants
2. How to Write a Business Plan
3. Secrets to making money on eBay
4. Credit Repair
5. Goal Setting
6. Asset Protection How to Incorporate

$10,000 MegaSized Internet Marketing &

Copy Writing & SEO Course &

$1,000 Value Bonus

Library III

1. SEO SIMPLIFIED PART 1

2. SEO SIMPLIFIED PART 2

3. SEO Private Network Blogs

4. SEO Social Signals

5. SEO Profits

Bonus 1000 Package!

1. Insider Secrets to Government Contracts (PDF)

2. 1000 Books/Guides (text files)

3. Vacation Discounts (text file w/links to discounts)

4. Media Players (3 Software Programs)

100% MONEY BACK GUARANTEE!!!

ALL ON A 8 GIGABYTE FLASH DRIVE

This Massive Library with a $10,000 value all for only a

1 time payment of $67!!!

Get Instant Access by Using the Link Below:

https://urlzs.com/p7v3T

Leave a review and join Our VIP Mailing List Then Get All our Audio Books Free! We will be releasing over 100 money making audio books within the next 12 months! Just leave a review and join our mailing list and get them all for free!

Just Hit/Type in the Link Below

https://urlzs.com/HfbGF

Please Leave a Review!

There is not another real estate investing book on the market that gives you as many sources for wholesale real estate than this book.

My book gives you more and in most cases for less!

This book also gives you a web site that has over 4,000 sources of real estate financing in addition to the government's over 2,400 sources of Federal Assistance.

I have enjoyed doing all the research and sharing my real world real estate investing experience in what I hope is easy to understand terminology.

So I ask you to leave a honest and hopefully great review!

Thank you.

Warm Regards,

www.ingramcontent.com/pod-product-compliance
Lightning Source LLC
Chambersburg PA
CBHW060933220326
41597CB00020BA/3820